MONEDAS Y BILLETES
COINS AND MONEY

DÓLARES
DOLLAR BILLS

ROBERT M. HAMILTON
TRADUCIDO POR ANA MARÍA GARCÍA

PowerKiDS
press.

New York

Published in 2016 by The Rosen Publishing Group, Inc.
29 East 21st Street, New York, NY 10010

First Edition

Editor: Katie Kawa
Book Design: Katelyn Heinle
Spanish Translator: Ana María García

Photo Credits: Cover, p. 1 (piggy bank) Lizzie Roberts/Ikon Images/Getty Images; cover, pp. 6, 9, 10, 13, 17, 18, 21, 22 (background design element) Paisit Teeraphatsakool/Shutterstock.com; cover, p. 1 (wavy dollar bill) Bragin Alexey/Shutterstock.com; cover, p. 1 (flat dollar bills) komkrit Preechachanwate/Shutterstock.com; p. 5 Andersen Ross/Iconica/Getty Images; pp. 6, 9, 10, 13 (dollar bill) Fablok/Shutterstock.com; pp. 6, 9, 10, 18 (vector bubbles) Dragan85/Shutterstock.com; p. 9 (pile of pennies) karen roach/Shutterstock.com; p. 10 (quarters) Courtesy of U.S. Mint; p. 13 (George Washington) © iStockphoto.com/joecicak; p. 14 Education Images/ UIG/Universal Images Group/Getty Images; p. 17 (vector bubble) gst/Shutterstock.com; pp. 17, 18, 24 (dollar bill reverse) Parhamr/Wikimedia Commons; pp. 21, 22 (vector bubble) LAN02/Shutterstock.com; p. 21 (money fan) Scorpp/Shutterstock.com; p. 22 (five-dollar bill) Robynrg/Shutterstock.com.

Library of Congress Cataloging-in-Publication Data

Hamilton, Robert M., 1987-
 Dollar bills = Dólares / Robert M. Hamilton.
    pages cm. — (Coins and money = Monedas y billetes)
Parallel title: Monedas y billetes.
In English and Spanish.
 Includes bibliographical references and index.
 ISBN 978-1-4994-0691-7 (library binding)
1. Paper money—Juvenile literature. 2. Dollar, American. I. Title.
 HG353.H36 2015
 332.4'0440973—dc23

Manufactured in the United States of America

CPSIA Compliance Information: Batch #WS15PK: For Further Information contact Rosen Publishing, New York, New York at 1-800-237-9932

CONTENIDO

CONTENTS

Los dólares son un tipo de dinero de papel. Utilizamos dinero para comprar cosas.

Dollar bills are a kind of paper money. We use money to buy things.

Los billetes tienen números que indican qué valor tienen. Un billete de un dólar vale un dólar.

Bills have numbers on them to show how much they are worth. A dollar bill is one dollar.

Un billete de un dólar es igual a 100 centavos. Esto quiere decir que es igual a 100 *pennies*.

One dollar bill is the same as 100 cents. This means it is the same as 100 pennies.

1 DÓLAR = **100 CENTAVOS**
1 DOLLAR = **100 PENNIES**

1 DÓLAR
1 DOLLAR

=

4 monedas de veinticinco centavos
4 QUARTERS

Un billete de un dólar equivale a cuatro monedas de veinticinco centavos.

One dollar bill is also the same as four quarters.

En la parte delantera del billete de un dólar hay un rostro de hombre. Es el Presidente George Washington.

The front of a dollar bill has a man's face on it. This is President George Washington.

George Washington fue el primer presidente de Estados Unidos. Por eso está en el billete de un dólar.

George Washington was the first president of the United States. This is why he is on the dollar bill.

En la parte de atrás del billete de un dólar se ve una **pirámide**. Tiene 13 escalones.

The back of a dollar bill has a **pyramid** on it. It has 13 steps.

En la parte de atrás del billete de un dólar también hay un **águila calva**. Es un símbolo de Estados Unidos.

The back of a dollar bill also has a **bald eagle** on it. This stands for the United States.

Algunos billetes son de más de un dólar.

Some bills are more than one dollar.

Este billete tiene impreso
el número 5. ¿Cuántos
dólares son?

This bill has the number 5 on it.
How many dollars is it?

PALABRAS QUE DEBES APRENDER
WORDS TO KNOW

(el) águila calva
bald eagle

(la) pirámide
pyramid

ÍNDICE / INDEX

SITIOS DE INTERNET / WEBSITES

Due to the changing nature of Internet links, PowerKids Press has developed an online list of websites related to the subject of this book. This site is updated regularly. Please use this link to access the list: www.powerkidslinks.com/cam/dol